The THEORY & PRACTICE of RIVERS

AND

NEW POEMS

The THEORY & PRACTICE of RIVERS

AND

NEW POEMS

by

JIM HARRISON

Illustrated by
RUSSELL CHATHAM

CLARK CITY PRESS
LIVINGSTON · MONTANA

ISBN 0–944439–13–6 [casebound]

ISBN 0–944439–10–1 [paperback]

LIBRARY OF CONGRESS NUMBER: 88–63676

Clark City Press

POST OFFICE BOX 1358

LIVINGSTON, MT 59047

CONTENTS

The THEORY *&* PRACTICE *of* RIVERS

NEW POEMS

The THEORY *&* PRACTICE *of* RIVERS

The rivers of my life:
moving looms of light,
anchored beneath the log
at night I can see the moon
up through the water
as shattered milk, the nudge
of fishes, belly and back
in turn grating against log
and bottom; and letting go, the current
lifts me up and out
into the dark, gathering motion,
drifting into an eddy
with a sideways swirl,
the sandbar cooler than the air:
to speak it clearly,
how the water goes
is how the earth is shaped.

It is not so much that I got
there from here, which is everyone's
story: but the shape
of the voyage, how it pushed
outward in every direction
until it stopped:
roots of plants and trees,
certain coral heads,
photos of splintered lightning,
blood vessels,
the shapes of creeks and rivers.

This is the ascent out of water:
there is no time but that
of convenience, time so that everything
won't happen at once; dark
doesn't fall—dark comes up
out of the earth, an exhalation.
It gathers itself close
to the ground, rising
to envelop us, as if the bottom
of the sea rose up to meet us.
Have you ever gone
to the bottom of the sea?

Mute unity of water.
I sculpted this girl
out of ice so beautifully
she was taken away.
How banal the swan song
which is a water song.
There never was a swan
who said goodbye. My raven
in the pine tree squawked his way
to death, falling from branch
to branch. To branch again.
To ground. The song, the muffle
of earth as the body falls,
feather against pine needles.

Near the estuary north of Guilford
my brother recites the Episcopalian
burial service over his dead daughter.
Gloria, as in *Gloria in excelsis*.
I cannot bear this passion and courage;
my eyes turn toward the swamp
and sea, so blurred they'll never quite
clear themselves again. The inside of the eye,
vitreous humor, is the same pulp found
inside the squid. I can see Gloria
in the snow and in the water. She lives
in the snow and water and in my eyes.
This is a song for her.

Kokoplele saved me this time:
flute song in soft dark
sound of water over rock,
the moon glitter rippling;
breath caught as my hunched
figure moved in a comic circle,
seven times around the cabin
through the woods in the dark.
Why did I decide to frighten myself?

Light snow in early May,
wolf prints in alluvial fan,
moving across the sandbar
in the river braided near its mouth
until the final twist; then the prints
move across drift ice in a dead
channel, and back into the swamp.

The closest I came to describing it:
it is early winter, mid-November
with light snow, the ground rock hard
with frost. We are moving but I can't
seem to find my wife and two daughters.
I have left our old house and can't remember
how to find the new one.

The days are stacked against
what we think we are:
the story of the water babies
swimming up and down stream
amid waterweed, twisting
with cherubic smiles in the current,
human and fish married.
Again! The girl I so painfully
sculpted out of ice
was taken away. She said:
"Goddamn the Lizard King,"
her night message and goodbye.
The days are stacked against
what we think we are:
near the raven rookery
inside the bend of river
with snow melt and rain
flooding the bend; I've failed to stalk
these birds again and they flutter
and wheel above me with parental screams
saying get out get out you bastard.
The days are stacked against
what we think we are.

After a month of interior weeping
it occurred to me in times like these
I have nothing to fall back on
except the sun and moon and earth.
I dress in camouflage and crawl
around swamps and forest, seeing
the bitch coyote five times but never
before she sees me. Her look
is curious, almost a smile.

The days are stacked against
what we think we are:
it is nearly impossible
to surprise ourselves.
I will never wake up
and be able to play the piano.

South fifteen miles, still
near the river, calling coyotes
with Dennis E: full moon in east
northern lights in pale green swirl,
from the west an immense line squall
and thunderstorm approaching off Lake Superior.
Failing with his call he uses
the song of the loon to bring
an answer from the coyotes.
"They can't resist it," he says.
The days are stacked against
what we think we are.
Standing in the river up to my waist
the infant beaver peeks at me
from the flooded tag alder
and approaches though warned
by her mother whacking her tail.
About seven feet away she bobs
to dive, mooning me with her small
pink ass, rising again for another
look, then downward swimming
past my leg, still looking.
The days are finally stacked
against what we think we are:
how long can I stare at the river?
Three months in a row now
with no signs of stopping,
glancing to the right, an almost
embarrassed feeling that the river
will stop flowing and I can go home.
The days, at last, are stacked against
what we think we are.

Who in their most hallowed, sleepless
night with the moon seven feet
outside the window, the moon
that the river swallows, would wish
it otherwise?

On New Year's Eve I'm wrapped
in my habits, looking up to the TV
to see the red ball, the apple,
rise or fall, I forget which:
a poem on the cherrywood table, a fire,
a blizzard, some whiskey, three
restless cats, and two sleeping dogs,
at home and making three gallons
of *menudo* for the revelers who'll
need it come tomorrow after amateur night:
about ten pounds of tripe, ancho,
molida, serrano, and chipotle pepper, cumin,
coriander, a few calves' or piglets' feet.
I don't wonder what is becoming
to the man already becoming.
I also added a half-quart of stock
left over from last night's *bollito misto*
wherein I poach for appropriate times:
fifteen pounds of veal bones to be discarded,
a beef brisket, a pork roast, Italian sausage,
a large barnyard hen, a pheasant, a guinea
hen, and for about thirty minutes until
rosy rare a whole filet, served with
three sauces: tomato coulis, piquante (anchovies & capers etc.)
and a rouille. Last week when my daughter

came home from NYC I made her venison
with truffles, also roast quail for Christmas
breakfast, also a wild turkey, some roast mallards & grouse,
also a cacciatore of rabbit & pheasant.
Oddly the best meal of the year
was in the cabin by the river:

a single fresh brook trout *au bleu*
with one boiled new potato and one
wild leek vinaigrette. By the river
I try to keep alive, perhaps to write
more poems, though lately I think
of us all as lay-down comedians
who, when we finally tried to get up,
have found that our feet are mushy,
and what's more, no one cares
or bothers to read anymore those
sotto voce below radar flights
from the empirical. But I am wrapped
in my habits. I must send my prayer

upward and downward. "Why do you write
poems?" the stewardess asked. "I guess
it's because every angel is terrible
still though, alas, I invoke these almost
deadly birds of the soul,"
I cribbed from Rilke.

The travels on dry riverbeds: Salt River,
or nearly dry up Canyon de Chelly,
a half-foot of water—a skin over
the brown river bed. The Navaho
family stuck with a load of dry
corn and crab apples. Only the woman
speaks English, the children at first shy
and frightened of my blind left eye
(some tribes attach importance to this—
strangely enough, this eye can see under water).
We're up on the del Muerto fork and while
I'm kneeling in the water shoving rocks
under the axle I glance skywards
at an Anasazi cliff dwelling, the "ancient
ones" they're called. This morning
a young schizophrenic Navaho attacked
our truck with a club, his head seeming
to turn nearly all the way around as
an owl's. Finally the children smile
as the truck is pulled free. I am given
a hatful of the most delicious crab apples
in the world. I watch the first apple
core float west on the slender current,
my throat a knot of everything
I no longer understand.

Sitting on the bank, the water
stares back so deeply you can hear
it afterwards when you wish. It is the water
of dreams, and for the nightwalker
who can almost walk on the water,
it is most of all the water of awakening,
passing with the speed of life
herself, drifting in circles in an eddy
joining the current again
as if the eddy were a few moments' sleep.

The story can't hesitate to stop.
I can't find a river in Los Angeles
except the cement one behind Sportsman's Lodge
on Ventura. There I feel my
high blood pressure like an electric tiara
around my head, a small comic cloud,
a miniature junkyard where my confused
desires, hopes, hates and loves short circuit
in little puffs of hissing ozone. And the women
are hard green horses disappearing,
concealing themselves in buildings and tops
of wild palms in ambush.
A riverless city of redolent
and banal sobs, green girls
in trees, girls hard as basalt.
"My grandfather screwed me
when I was seven years old,"
she said, while I looked out
at the cement river flowing with dusty rain,
at three dogs playing in the cement river.

"He's dead now so there's no point
sweating it," she added.

Up in the Amazon River Basin
during a dark time Matthiessen built
a raft with a native, chewed some coca leaves,
boarded the raft and off they went on a river
not on any map, uncharted, wanting to see
the Great Mother of Snakes; a truncated
version of our voyage of seventy years—
actuarial average. To see green and live green,
moving on water sometimes clouded often clear.
Now our own pond is white with ice.
In the barnyard lying in the snow
I can hear the underground creek,
a creek without a name.

I forgot to tell you that while
I was away my heart broke
and I became not so much old, but older,
definably older within a few days.
This happened on a cold dawn in New Iberia
while I was feeding a frightened, stray
dog a sack of pork rinds in the rain.

Three girls danced the Cotton-eyed Joe,
almost sedate, erect, with relentless grace,
where did they come from
and where did they go

in ever so delicate circles?
And because of time, circles
that no longer close
or return to themselves.

I rode the grey horse
all day in the rain.
The fields became unmoving rivers,
the trees foreshortened.
I saw a girl in a white dress
standing half-hidden in the water
behind a maple tree.
I pretended not to notice
and made a long slow circle
behind a floating hedge top
to catch her unawares.
She was gone but I had that prickly
fear someone was watching from a tree,
far up in a leaf-veil of green maple leaves.
Now the horse began swimming
toward higher ground, from where
I watched the tree until dark.

"Life, this vastly mysterious process
to which our culture inures us
lest we become useless citizens!
And is it terrible to be lonely and ill?"
she wrote. "Not at all, in fact, it is better
to be lonely when ill. To others, friends,
relatives, loved ones, death is our most
interesting, our most dramatic act.
Perhaps the best thing I've learned
from these apparently cursed and bedraggled
Indians I've studied all these years
is how to die. Last year I sat beside
a seven-year-old Hopi girl as she sang
her death song in a slight quavering
voice. Who among us whites, child
or adult, will sing while we die?"

On White Fish Bay, the motor broke down
in heavy seas. We chopped ice off the gunwales
quite happily as it was unlikely we'd survive
and it was something to do. Ted just sat there
out of the wind and spray drinking whiskey.
"I been on the wagon for a year. If I'm going
to die by god at least I get to have a drink."
What is it to actually go outside the nest
we have built for ourselves, and earlier
our father's nest: to go into a forest
alone with our eyes open? It's different
when you don't know what's over the hill—
keep the river on your left, then you see
the river on your right. I have simply
forgotten left and right, even up and down,

whirl then sleep on a cloudy day to forget
direction. It is hard to learn how
to be lost after so much training.

In New York I clocked
seven tugboats on the East River
in less than a half hour;
then I went to a party
where very rich people
talked about their arches,
foot arches, not architectural arches.
Back at my post I dozed
and saw only one more tugboat
before I slept.

But in New York I also saw a big hole
of maddened pipes with all the direction
of the swastika and a few immigrants
figuring it all out with the impenetrable
good sense of those who do the actual
work of the world.

How did I forget that rich turbulent
river, so cold in the rumply brown folds
of spring; by August cool, clear, glittery
in the sunlight; umbrous as it dips
under the logjam. In May, the river
a roar beyond a thin wall of sleep, with
the world of snow still gliding in rivulets
down imperceptible slopes; in August

through the screened window against which
bugs and moths scratch so lightly,
as lightly as the river sounds.

How can I renew oaths
I can't quite remember?
In New Orleans I was light in body and soul
because of food poisoning, the bathroom gymnastics
of flesh against marble floor,
seeing the underside of the bathtub
for the first time since I was a child,
and the next day crossing Cajun bridges
in the Atchafalaya, where blacks were thrown
to alligators I'm told, black souls whirling
in brown water, whirling
in an immaculate crawfish
rosary.

In the water I can remember
women I didn't know: Adriana
dancing her way home at the end
of a rope, a cool Tuscany night,
the apple tree in bloom;
the moon which I checked
was not quite full, a half-moon,
the rest of the life abandoned to the dark.

I warned myself all night
but then halfway between my ears
I turned toward the heavens
and reached the top of my head.
From there I can go just about
anywhere I want and I've never
found my way back home.

This isn't the old song
of the suicidal house,
I forgot the tune about small
windows growing smaller, the door
neither big enough to enter
or exit, the sinking hydraulic ceilings
and the attic full of wet cement.
I wanted to go to the Camargue,
to Corsica, to return to Costa Rica,
but I couldn't escape the suicidal house
until May when I drove
through the snow to reach the river.

On the bank by the spring creek
my shadow seemed to leap
up to gather me, or it leapt
up to gather me, not seeming so
but as a natural fact. Faulkner said
that the drowned man's shadow had watched
him from the river all the time.

Drowning in the bourgeois trough,
a *bourride* or gruel of money, drugs,
whiskey, hotels, the dream coasts,
ass in air at the trough, drowning
in a river of pus, pus of civilization,
pus of cities, unholy river of shit,
of filth, shit of nightmares, shit
of skewed dreams and swallowed years.
The river pulls me out,
draws me elsewhere
and down to blue water,
green water,
black water.

How far between the Virgin
and the Garrison and back?
Why is it a hundred times further to get back,
the return upriver in the dark?
It isn't innocence but to win back breath,
body heat, the light that gathers around
a waking animal. Ten years ago I saw
the dancing Virgin in a basement
in New York, a whirl of hot color
from floor to ceiling, whirling in a dance.
At eighteen in New York
on Grove Street I discovered
red wine, garlic, Rimbaud,
and a red-haired girl. Livid colors
not known in farm country,
also Charlie Parker, Sonny Rollins,
the odors from restaurant vents,
thirty-five cent Italian sausages

on MacDougal, and the Hudson River:
days of river watching and trying
to get on a boat for the tropics and see
that Great Ocean river, the Gulf Stream.
Another fifteen years before I saw
the Ocean river and the sharks hanging
under the sargassum weed lines,
a blue river in green water,
and the sharks staring back, sinking
down listlessly into darker water;
the torpor of heat, a hundred low tide
nights begging a forgetfulness
I haven't quite earned.

I forgot where I heard that poems
are designed to waken sleeping gods;
in our time they've taken on nearly
unrecognizable shapes as gods will do;
one is a dog, one is a scarecrow
that doesn't work—crows perch
on the wind-whipped sleeves,
one is a carpenter who doesn't become Jesus,
one is a girl who went to heaven
sixty years early. Gods die,
and not always out of choice,
like near-sighted cats jumping
between buildings seven stories up.
One god drew feathers out of my skin
so I could fly, a favor close to terror.
But this isn't a map of the gods.
When they live in rivers
it's because rivers have no equilibrium;

gods resent equilibrium when everything
that lives, *moves;* boulders
are a war of atoms, and the dandelion
cracks upward through the blacktop road.
Seltzer's tropical beetle grew
from a larval lump in a man's arm,
emerging full grown, pincers waving.
On Mt. Cuchama there were so many
gods passing through I hid in a hole
in a rock, waking one by accident.
I fled with a tight ass and cold skin.
I could draw a map of this place
but they're never caught in the same location
twice. And their voices change from involuntary
screams to the singular wail of the loon,
possibly the wind that can howl down Wall St.
Gods have long abandoned the banality of war
though they were stirred by a hundred-year-old
guitarist I heard in Brazil, also the autistic child
at the piano. We'll be greeted at death
so why should I wait? Today I invoked
any available god back in the woods in the fog.
The world was white with last week's melting
blizzard, the fog drifting upward, then descending.
The only sound was a porcupine eating bark
off an old tree, and a rivulet beneath the snow.
Sometimes the obvious is true: the full
moon on her bare bottom by the river!
For the gay, the full moon on the lover's prick!
Gods laugh at the fiction of gender.
Water gods, moon gods, god fever,
sun gods, fire gods, give this earth diver
more songs before I die.

22

A "system" suggests the cutting off,
i.e., in channel morphology, the reduction,
the suppression of texture to simplify:
to understand a man, or woman, growing
old with eagerness you first consider
the sensuality of death, an unacknowledged
surprise to most. In nature the physiology

23

has heat and color, beast and tree
saying aloud the wonder of death;
to study rivers, including the postcard
waterfalls, is to adopt another life;
a limited life attaches itself to the endless
movement, the renowned underground
rivers of South America which I've felt
thundering far beneath my feet—to die
is to descend into such rivers and flow
along in the perfect dark. But above ground
I'm memorizing life, from the winter moon
to the sound of my exhaustion in March
when all the sodden plans have collapsed
and only daughters, the dogs and cats
keep one from disappearing at gunpoint.
I brought myself here and stare nose to nose
at the tolerant cat who laps whiskey
from my mustache. Life often shatters
in schizoid splinters. I will avoid
becoming the cold stone wall I am straddling.

I had forgot what it was I liked
about life. I hear if you own a chimpanzee
they cease at a point to be funny. Writers
and politicians share an embarrassed moment
when they are sure all problems will disappear
if you get the language right.
That's not all they share—in each other's
company they are like boys who have been
discovered at wiener play in the toilet.
At worst, it's the gift of gab.
At best it's Martin Luther King and Rimbaud.

Bearing down hard on love and death
there is an equal and opposite reaction.
All these years they have split the pie,
leaving the topping for preachers
who don't want folks to fuck or eat.
What kind of magic, or rite of fertility,
to transcend this shit-soaked stew?

The river is as far as I can move
from the world of numbers: I'm all
for full retreats, escapes, a 47 yr. old runaway.
"Gettin' too old to run away," I wrote
but not quite believing this option is grey.
I stare into the deepest pool of the river
which holds the mystery of a cellar to a child,
and think of those two track-roads that dwindle
into nothing in the forest. I have this feeling
of walking around for days with the wind
knocked out of me. In the cellar was a root
cellar where we stored potatoes, apples, carrots
and where a family of harmless black snakes lived.
In certain rivers there are pools a hundred
foot deep. In a swamp I must keep secret
there is a deep boiling spring around which
in the dog days of August large brook trout
swim and feed. An adult can speak dreams
to children saying that there is a spring
that goes down to the center of the earth.
Maybe there is. Next summer I'm designing
and building a small river about seventy-seven
foot long. It will flow both ways, in reverse
of nature. I will build a dam and blow it up.

25

The involuntary image that sweeps
into the mind, irresistible and without evident
cause as a dream or thunderstorm,
or rising to the surface from childhood,
the longest journey taken in a split second,
from there to now, without pause:

26

in the woods with Mary Cooper, my first love
wearing a voilet scarf in May. We're
looking after her huge mongoloid aunt,
trailing after this woman who loves us
but so dimly perceives the world. We pick
and clean wild leeks for her. The creek
is wild and dangerous with the last
of the snowmelt. The child-woman
tries to enter the creek and we tackle her.
She's stronger, then slowly understands,
half-wet and muddy. She kisses me
while Mary laughs, then Mary kisses me
over and over. Now I see the pools
in the Mongol eyes that watch and smile
with delight and hear the roar of the creek,
smell the scent of leeks on her muddy lips.

This is an obscene Koan set plumb
in the middle of the Occident:
the man with three hands lacks symmetry
but claps the loudest, the chicken
in circles on the sideless road, a plane
that takes off and can never land.
I am not quite alert enough to live.
The fallen nest and fire in the closet,
my world without guardrails, the electric
noose, the puddle that had no bottom.
The fish in underground rivers are white
and blind as the porpoises who live far up
the muddy Amazon. In New York and L.A.
you don't want to see, hear, smell,
and you only open your mouth in restaurants.

At night you touch people with rock-hard skins.
I'm trying to become alert enough to live.
Yesterday after the blizzard I hiked far back
in a new swamp and found an iceless
pond connected to the river by a small creek.
Against deep white snow and black trees
there was a sulphurous fumarole, rank and sharp
in cold air. The water bubbled up brown,
then spread in turquoise to deep black,
without the track of a single mammal to drink.
This was nature's own, a beauty too strong
for life; a place to drown not live.

On waking after the accident
I was presented with the "whole picture"
as they say, magnificently detailed,
a child's diorama of what life appears to be:
staring at the picture I became drowsy
with relief when I noticed a yellow
dot of light in the lower right-hand corner.
I unhooked the machines and tubes and crawled
to the picture, with an eyeball to the dot
of light which turned out to be a miniature
tunnel at the end of which I could see
mountains and stars whirling and tumbling,
sheets of emotions, vertical rivers, upside
down lakes, herds of unknown mammals, birds
shedding feathers and regrowing them instantly,
snakes with feathered heads eating their own
shed skins, fish swimming straight up,
the bottom of Isaiah's robe, live whales
on dry ground, lions drinking from a golden

bowl of milk, the rush of night,
and somewhere in this the murmur of gods—
a tree-rubbing-tree music, a sweet howl
of water and rock-grating-rock, fire
hissing from fissures, the moon settled
comfortably on the ground, beginning to roll.

KOBUN

Hotei didn't need a zafu,
saying that his ass was sufficient.
The head's a cloud anchor
that the feet must follow.
Travel light, he said,
or don't travel at all.

LOOKING FORWARD TO AGE

I will walk down to a marina
on a hot day and not go out to sea.

I will go to bed and get up early,
and carry too much cash in my wallet.

On Memorial Day I will visit the graves
of all those who died in my novels.

If I have become famous I'll wear a green
janitor's suit and row a wooden boat.

From a key ring on my belt will hang
thirty-three keys that open no doors.

Perhaps I'll take all of my grandchildren
to Disneyland in a camper but probably not.

One day standing in a river with my flyrod
I'll have the courage to admit my life.

In a one-room cabin at night I'll consign
photos, all tentative memories to the fire.

And you my loves, few as there have been, let's lie
and say it could never have been otherwise.

So that: we may glide off in peace, not howling
like orphans in this endless century of war.

These simple rules to live within—a black
pen at night, a gold pen in daylight,
avoid blue food and ten-ounce shots
of whiskey, don't point a gun at yourself,
don't snipe with the cri-cri-cri of a *becasine*,
don't use gas for starter fluid, don't read
dirty magazines in front of stewardesses—
it happens all the time; it's time to stop
cleaning your plate, forget the birthdays
of the dead, give all you can to the poor.
This might go on and on and will: who can
choose between the animal in the road
and the ditch? A magnum for lunch
is a little too much but not enough
for dinner. Polish the actual stars at night
as an invisible man pets a dog, an actual
man a memory-dog lost under
the morning glory trellis forty years ago.
Dance with yourself with all your heart
and soul, and occasionally others, but don't
eat all the berries birds eat or you'll die.
Kiss yourself in the mirror but don't fall in love
with photos of ladies in magazines. Don't fall
in love as if you were falling through
the floor in an abandoned house, or off
a dock at night, or down a crevasse
covered with false snow, a cow floundering
in quicksand while the other cows watch
without particular interest, backwards
off a crumbling cornice. Don't fall in love
with two at once. From the ceiling you can see
this circle of three, though one might be elsewhere.

He is rended, he rends himself, he dances,
he whirls so hard everything he *is* flies off.
He crumples as paper but rises daily from the dead.

That hot desert beach in Ecuador,
with scarcely a splotch of vegetation
fronting as it does
a Pacific so immensely lush
it hurls lobsters on great flat
boulders where children brave fatal
waves to pick them up.
Turning from one to the other quickly,
it is incomprehensible: from wild, grey
sunblasted burro eating cactus to azure
immensity of ocean, from miniature
goat dead on infantile feet in sand
to imponderable roar of swells, equatorial sun;
music that squeezes the blood out of the heart
by midnight, and girls whose legs
glisten with sweat, their teeth white
as Canadian snow, legs pounding as plump
brown pistons, and night noises I've
never heard, though at the coolest period
in these latitudes, near the faintest
beginning of dawn, there was the cold
unmistakable machine gun, the harshest
chatter death can make. Only then do
I think of my very distant relative, Lorca,
that precocious skeleton, as he crumpled
earthwards against brown pine needles;
and the sky, vaster than the Pacific,
whirled overhead, a sky without birds or clouds,
azul te quiero azul.

March 5: first day without a fire.
Too early. Too early. Too early!
Take joy in the day
without consideration, the three
newly-brought-to-life bugs
who are not meant to know
what they are doing avoid each other
on a window stained
by a dozen storms.

We eat our father's food:
herring, beans, salt pork,
sauerkraut, pig hocks, salt cod.
I have said goodbye with one thousand
laments so that even the heart of the rose
becomes empty as my dog's rubber ball.
The dead are not meant to go,
but to trail off so that one can
see them on a distant hillock,
across the river, in dreams
from which one awakens nearly healed:
don't worry, it's fine to be dead,
they say; we were a little early
but could not help ourselves.
Everyone dies as the child they were,
and at that moment, this secret,
intricately concealed heart blooms

forth with the first song anyone
sang in the dark, "now I lay me
down to sleep, I pray the Lord
my soul to keep. . . ."

Now this oddly gentle winter, almost dulcet,
winds to a blurred close with trees full
of birds that belong further south,
and people are missing something
to complain about; a violent March
is an unacknowledged prayer;
a rape of nature, a healing blizzard,
a very near disaster.

So this last lament:
as unknowable as the eye of the crow
staring down from the walnut tree,
blind as the Magellanic clouds,
as cold as that March mud puddle
at the foot of the granary steps,
unseeable as the birthright of the L. A.
whore's Nebraska childhood of lilacs
and cornfields and an unnamed prairie
bird that lived in a thicket
where she hid,
as treacherous as a pond's spring
ice to a child,
black as the scar of a half-peeled
birch tree,
the wrench of the beast's heart just
short of the waterhole,
as bell-clear as a gunshot at dawn,
is the ache of a father's death.

It is that, but far more:
as if we take a voyage out of life
as surely as we took a voyage in,
almost as frightened children
in a cellar's cold grey air;
or before memory—they put me on a boat
on this river, then I was lifted off;
in our hearts, it is always just after
dawn, and each bird's song is the first,
and that ever so slight breeze that touches
the tops of trees and ripples the lake
moves through our bodies as if we were gods.

HORSE

What if it were our privilege
to sculpt our dreams of animals?
But those shapes in the night
come and go too quickly to be held
in stone: but not to avoid these shapes
as if dreams were only a nighttime
pocket to be remembered and avoided.
Who can say in the depths of
his life and heart what beast
most stopped life, the animals
he watched, the animals he only touched
in dreams? Even our hearts don't beat
the way we want them to. What
can we know in that waking,
sleeping edge? We put down
my daughter's old horse, old and
arthritic, a home burial. By dawn with eye
half-open, I said to myself, is
he still running, is he still running
around, under the ground?

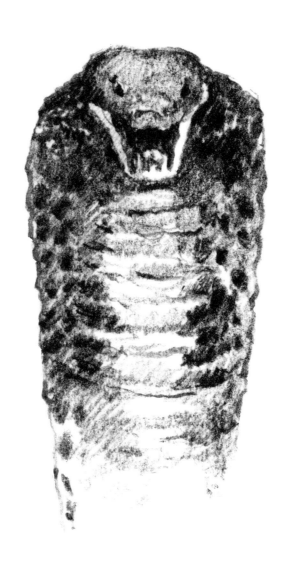

COBRA

What are these nightmares,
so wildly colored? We're in every
movie we see, even in our sleep.
Not that we can become what
we fear most but that we can't
resist ourselves. The grizzly
attack; after that divorce
and standing outside the school
with a rifle so they can't take my
daughter, Anna. By god! Long ago
in Kenya where I examined the
grass closely before I sat down
to a poisonous lunch, I worried
about cobras. When going insane I worried
about cobra venom in Major Grey's Chutney.
Simple as that. Then in overnight sleep I became
a lordly cobra, feeling the pasture grass
at high noon glide beneath my
stomach. I watched the house with
my head arched above the weeds,
then slept in the cool dirt under the granary.

Every year, when we're fly fishing for tarpon
off Key West, Guy insists that porpoises
are good luck. But it's not so banal
as catching more fish or having a fashion
model fall out of the sky lightly on your head,
or at your feet depending on certain
preferences. It's what porpoises do to the ocean.
You see a school making love off Boca Grande,
the baby with his question mark staring
at us a few feet from the boat.
Porpoises dance for as long as they live.
You can do nothing for them.
They alter the universe.

THE BRAND NEW STATUE OF LIBERTY
to Lee Iacocca (another Michigan boy)

I was commissioned in a dream by Imanja,
also the black pope of Brazil, Tancred,
to design a seven-tiered necklace
of seven thousand skulls for the Statue of Liberty.
Of course from a distance they'll look
like pearls, but in November
when the strongest winds blow, the skulls
will rattle wildly, bone against metal,
a crack and chatter of bone against metal,
the true sound of history, this metal striking bone.
I'm not going to get heavy-handed—
a job is a job and I've leased a football
field for the summer, gathered a group of ladies
who are art lovers, leased in advance
a bull Sikorsky freight helicopter
to drop on the necklace: funding comes
from Ford Foundation, Rockefeller, the N.E.A.
There is one Jewish skull from Atlanta, two
from Mississippi, but this is basically
an indigenous cast except skulls from tribes
of blacks who got a free ride over from Africa,
representative skulls from all the Indian
tribes, an assortment of grizzly, wolf,
coyote and buffalo skulls. But what beauty
when the morning summer sun glances
off these bony pates! And her great
iron lips quivering in a smile, almost a smirk
so that she'll drop the torch to fondle the jewels.

THE TIMES ATLAS

For my mentor, long dead, Richard
Halliburton and his Seven League Boots.

Today was the coldest day in the history
of the Midwest. Thank god for the moon
in this terrible storm.

There are areas far out at sea where
it rains a great deal. Camus said
it rained so hard even the sea was wet.

O god all our continents are only rifted
magma welled up from below. We don't
have a solid place to stand.

A little bullshit here as the Nile
is purportedly 80 miles longer
than the Amazon. I proclaim it a tie.

Pay out your 125 bucks and find out the world
isn't what you think it is but what
it is. We whirl so nothing falls off.
Eels, polar bears, bugs and men enjoy

the maker's design. No one really
leaves this place. O loveliness
of Caribbean sun off water under
trade wind's lilt.

Meanwhile the weather is no longer amusing.
Earth frightens me, the blizzard, house's
shudder, Oceanic roar, the brittle night
that might leave so many dead.

NEW POEMS

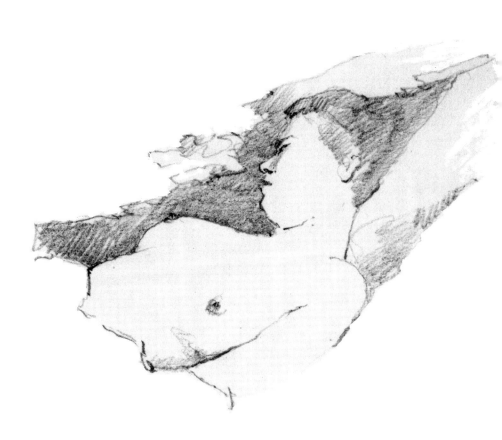

NEW LOVE

With these dire portents
we'll learn the language
of knees, shoulder blades,
chins but not the first floor up,
shin bones, the incomprehensible
belly buttons of childhood,
heels and the soles of our feet,
spines and neckbones,
risque photos of the tender
inside of elbows, tumescent fingers
draw the outlines of lost parts
on the wall; bottom and pubis
Delphic, unapproachable as Jupiter,
a memory worn as the first love
we knew, ourselves a test pattern
become obsession: this love
in the plague years—we used to kiss
a mirror to see if we were dead.
Now we relearn the future as we learned
to walk, as a baby grabs its toes,
tilts backward, rocking. Tonight I'll touch
your wrist and in a year perhaps grind
my blind eye's socket against your hipbone.
With all this death, behind our backs,
the moon has become the moon again.

August, a dense heat wave at the cabin
mixed with torrents of rain,
the two-tracks become miniature rivers.

In the Russian Orthodox Church
one does not talk to God, one sings.
This empty and sun-blasted land

has a voice rising in shimmers.
I did not sing in Moscow
but St. Basil's in Leningrad raised

a quiet tune. But now seven worlds
away I hang the *cazas-moscas*
from the ceiling and catch seven flies

in the first hour, buzzing madly
against the stickiness. I've never seen
the scissor-tailed flycatcher, a favorite

bird of my youth, the worn Audubon
card pinned to the wall. When I miss
flies three times with the swatter

they go free for good. Fair is fair.
There is too much nature pressing against
the window as if it were a green night;

and the river swirling in glazed turbulence
is less friendly than ever before.
Forty years ago she called come home, come home,

it's suppertime. I was fishing a fishless
cattle pond with a new three-dollar pole,
dreaming the dark blue ocean of pictures.

In the barn I threw down hay
while my Swede grandpa finished milking,
squirting the barn cat's mouth with an udder.

I kissed the wet nose of my favorite cow,
drank a dipper of fresh warm milk
and carried two pails to the house,

scraping the manure off my feet
in the pump shed. She poured the milk
in the cream separator and I began cranking.

At supper the oil cloth was decorated
with worn pink roses. We ate cold herring,
also the bluegills we had caught at daylight.

The fly-strip above the table idled in
the window's breeze, a new fly in its death buzz.
Grandpa said, "We are all flies."

That's what he said forty years ago.

ACTING
for J.N.

In the best sense,
becoming another
so that there is no trace left
of what we think is the self.
I am whomever.
It is not gesture
but the cortex of gesture,
not movement
but the soul of movement.
Look at the earth with your left eye
and at the sky with your right.
Worship contraries.
What makes us alike
is also what makes us different.
From Man to Jokester to Trickster
is a nudge toward the deep,
the incalculable abyss
you stare into so it will
stare back into you.
We are our consciousness
and it is the god in us
who struggles to be in everyone
in order to be ourselves.
When you see the chalked form
of the murdered man on the cement
throw yourself onto it and feel
the heat of the stone-hard fit.
This is the liquid poem,
the forefinger traced around both
the neck and the sun:

to be and be and be
as a creek turns corners
by grace of volume, heft of water,
speed by rate of drop,
even the contour of stone
changing day by day.
So that: when you wake in the night,
the freedom of the nightmare
turned to dream follows you
into morning, and there is no
skin on earth you cannot enter,
no beast or plant,
no man or woman
you may not flow through
and become.

MY FRIEND THE BEAR

Down in the bone myth of the cellar
of this farmhouse, behind the empty fruit jars
the whole wall swings open to the room
where I keep the bear. There's a tunnel
to the outside on the far wall that emerges
in the lilac grove in the backyard
but she rarely uses it, knowing there's no room
around here for a freewheeling bear.
She's not a dainty eater so once a day
I shovel shit while she lopes in playful circles.
Privately she likes religion—from the bedroom
I hear her incantatory moans and howls
below me—and April 23rd, when I open
the car trunk and whistle at midnight
and she shoots up the tunnel, almost airborne
when she meets the night. We head north
and her growls are less friendly as she scents
the forest above the road smell. I release
her where I found her as an orphan three
years ago, bawling against the dead carcass
of her mother. I let her go at the head
of the gully leading down to the swamp,
jumping free of her snarls and roars.
But each October 9th, one day before bear season
she reappears at the cabin, frightening
the bird dogs. We embrace ear to ear,
her huge head on my shoulder,
her breathing like god's.

CABIN POEM

I

The blonde girl
with a polka heart:
one foot, then another,
then aerial
in a twisting jump,
chin upward
with a scream of such
splendor
I go back to my cabin,
and start a fire.

II

Art & life
drunk & sober
empty & full
guilt & grace
cabin & home
north & south
struggle & peace
after which we catch
a glimpse of stars,
the white glistening pelt
of the Milky Way,
hear the startled bear crashing
through the delta swamp below me.
In these troubled times
I go inside and start a fire.

III

I am the bird that hears the worm,
or, my cousin said, the pulse of a wound
that probes to the opposite side.
I have abandoned alcohol, cocaine,
the news, and outdoor prayer
as support systems.
How can you make a case for yourself
before an ocean of trees, or standing
waist-deep in the river? Or sitting
on the logjam with a pistol?
I reject oneness with bears.
She has two cubs and thinks she
owns the swamp I thought I bought.
I shoot once in the air to tell her
it's my turn at the logjam
for an hour's thought about nothing.
Perhaps that is oneness with bears.
I've decided to make up my mind
about nothing, to assume the water mask,
to finish my life disguised as a creek,
an eddy, joining at night the full,
sweet flow, to absorb the sky,
to swallow the heat and cold, the moon
and the stars, to swallow myself
in ceaseless flow.

RICH FOLKS, POOR FOLKS, AND NEITHER

I

Rich folks keep their teeth
until late in life,
and park their cars in heated garages.
They own kitsch statues of praying hands
that conceal seven pounds of solid gold,
knowing that burglars hedge at icons.
At the merest twinge they go to the dentist,
and their dogs' anuses are professionally
inspected for unsuspected diseases.
Rich folks dream of the perfect massage
that will bring secret, effortless orgasm,
and absolutely super and undiscovered
islands with first-rate hotels
where they will learn to windsurf
in five minutes. They buy clothes that fit—
a forty waist means forty pants—rich folks
don't squeeze into thirty-eights. At spas
they are not too critical of their big asses,
and they believe in real small portions
because they can eat again pretty quick.
Rich folks resent richer folks
and they also resent poor folks
for their failures at meniality.
It's unfortunate for our theory that the same
proportion of rich folks are pleasant
as poor folks, a pitiless seven
percent, though not necessarily the ones

who still say their prayers and finish
the morning oatmeal to help the poor.
Everyone I have ever met is deeply
puzzled.

II

Up in Michigan poor folks dream of trips
to Hawaii or "Vegas." They muttered deeply
when the banker won the big lottery—
"It just don't seem fair," they said.
Long ago when I was poor
there was something in me that craved
to get fired, to drink a shot and beer
with a lump in my throat, hitchhike
or drive to California in an old car,
tell my family "I'll write if I get work."
In California, where you can sleep outside
every night, I saw the Pacific Ocean
and ate my first food of the Orient,
a fifty-cent bowl of noodles and pork.
No more cornmeal mush with salt pork
gravy, no more shovels at dawn,
no more clothes smelling of kerosene,
no more girls wearing ankle bracelets spelling
another's name. No more three hour waits
in unemployment lines, or cafeteria catsup
and bread for fifteen cents. I've eaten
my last White Tower burger and I'm heading
for the top. Or not. How could I dream
I'd end up moist-eyed in the Beverly Hills Hotel

when I ordered thirteen appetizers for myself
and the wheels of the laden trolley squeaked?
The television in the limousine broke down
and I missed the news on the way to look
at the ocean where there were no waves.
When I went bankrupt I began to notice cemeteries
and wore out my clothes, drank up the wine cellar.
I went to the movies and kissed my wife a lot
for the same reason—they're both in technicolor.
Everyone I met in those days was deeply puzzled.

III

Now I've rubbed rich and poor together
like two grating stones, mixed them temporarily
like oil and vinegar, male and female, until
my interest has waned to nothing. One night I saw
a constellation that chose not to reappear,
drifting in the day into another galaxy.
I tried to ignore the sound of my footsteps
in the woods until I did, and when I swam
in the river I finally forgot it was water,
but I still can't see a cow without saying cow.
Perhaps this was not meant to be. I dug
a deep hole out in a clearing in the forest
and sat down in it, studying the map
of the sky above me for clues, a new bible.
This is rushing things a bit, I thought.
I became a woman then became a man again.
I hiked during the night alone and gave
my dogs fresh bones until they no longer cared.
I bought drinks for the poor and for myself,

left mail unopened, didn't speak on the phone,
only listened. I shot the copy machine with my rifle.
No more copies, I thought, everything original!
Now I am trying to unlearn the universe
in the usual increments of nights and days.
Time herself often visits in swirling but gentle clouds.

Way out there on the borders of my consciousness
I've caught glimpses of that great dark bird,
the beating of whose wings is death, drawing closer.
How could it be otherwise? I thought.
Down in the hole last August during a thunderstorm
I watched her left wing tip shudder past
between two lightning strokes. Maybe I'll see her again
during the northern lights, but then, at that moment
I was still a child of water and mud.

DANCING

After the passing of irresistible
music you must learn to make
do with a dripping faucet,
rain or sleet on the roof,
eventually snow,
a cat's sigh,
the spherical notes that float
down from Aldebaran,
your cells as they part,
craving oxygen.

THE IDEA OF BALANCE IS TO BE FOUND
IN HERONS AND LOONS

I just heard a loon call on a TV ad
and my body gave itself
a quite voluntary shudder,
as in the night in East Africa
I heard the immense barking cough
of a lion, so foreign and indifferent.

But the lion drifts away
and the loon stays close,
calling as she did in my childhood,
in the cold rain a song
that tells the world of men
to keep its distance.

It isn't the signal of another life
or the reminder of anything
except her call: still,
at this quiet point past midnight
the rain is the same rain
that fell so long ago, and the loon
says I'm seven years old again.

*At the far ends of the lake
where no one lives or visits—
there are no roads to get there;
you take the watercourse way,*

the quiet drip and drizzle
of oars, slight squeak of oarlock,
the bare feet can feel the cold water
move beneath the old wood boat.

At one end the lordly, great blue herons
nest at the top of the white pine;
at the other end the loons,
just after daylight in cream-colored mist,
drifting with wails that begin as queru-
lous,
rising then into the spheres in volume,
with lost or doomed angels imprisoned
within their breasts.

SMALL POEM

There's something I've never known
when I get up in the morning.
Dead children fly off in the shape
of question marks, the doe's backward
glance at the stillborn fawn.
I don't know what it is
in the morning, as if incomprehension
beds down with me on waking.
What is the precise emotional temperature
when the young man hangs himself
in the jail cell with his father's belt?
What is the foot size of the Beast of Belsen?
This man in his over-remembered life
needs to know the source of the ache
which is an answer without a question,
his fingers wrapped around the memory
of life, as Cleopatra's around the snake's neck,
a shepherd's crook of love.

As a child, fresh out of the hospital
with tape covering the left side
of my face, I began to count birds.
At age fifty the sum total is precise
and astonishing, my only secret.
Some men count women or the cars
they've owned, their shirts—
long sleeved and short sleeved—
or shoes, but I have my birds,
excluding, of course, those extraordinary
days: the twenty-one thousand
snow geese and sandhill cranes at
Bosque del Apache; the sky blinded
by great frigate birds in the Pacific
off Anconcito, Ecuador; the twenty-one
thousand pink flamingos in Ngorongoro Crater
in Tanzania; the vast flock of sea birds
on the Seri coast of the Sea of Cortez
down in Sonora that left at nightfall,
then reappeared, resuming
their exact positions at dawn;
the one thousand cliff swallows nesting
in the sand cliffs of Pyramid Point,
their small round burrows like eyes,
really the souls of the Anasazi who flew
here a thousand years ago
to wait the coming of the Manitou.
And then there were the usual, almost deadly
birds of the soul—the crow with silver
harness I rode one night as if she
were a black, feathered angel;

the birds I became to escape unfortunate
circumstances—how the skin ached
as the feathers shot out toward light;
the thousand birds the dogs helped
me shoot to become a bird (grouse, woodcock,
duck, dove, snipe, pheasant, prairie chicken, etc.).
On my deathbed I'll write this secret
number on a slip of paper and pass
it to my wife and two daughters.
It will be a hot evening in late June
and they might be glancing out the window
at the thunderstorm's approach from the west.
Looking past their eyes and a dead fly
on the window screen I'll wonder
if there's a bird waiting for me in the onrushing clouds.
O birds, I'll sing to myself, you've carried
me along on this bloody voyage,
carry me now into that cloud,
into the marvel of this final night.

JIM HARRISON HAS PUBLISHED SEVERAL VOLUMES OF POETRY,
A COLLECTION OF NOVELLAS (*LEGENDS OF THE FALL*), AND
SIX NOVELS, THE MOST RECENT OF WHICH WAS *DALVA*. HE
LIVES WITH HIS FAMILY ON A FARM IN NORTHERN MICHIGAN.

INTERIOR ILLUSTRATIONS AND COVER PAINTING,
RIVER AT TWILIGHT, BY RUSSELL CHATHAM.
COVER DESIGN BY ANNE GARNER.
TYPE DESIGN BY ANNE GARNER AND SCOTT FREUTEL.
BOOK DESIGN BY JAMIE HARRISON POTENBERG.
COMPOSED IN ALDUS TYPES BY WILSTED & TAYLOR, OAKLAND.
PRINTED AND BOUND BY BRAUN-BRUMFIELD, INC., ANN ARBOR.